Loving and Letting Go

For parents who decided to turn away from aggressive medical intervention for their critically ill newborn

By Deborah L. Davis, Ph.D.

Design by Janet Sieff, Centering Corporation
Original artwork by Shari Borum

ISBN: 1-56123-060-X

Revised 2002
June

Additional copies and other grief resources
are available through the Centering Corporation.
Contact:
Centering Corporation
PO Box 4600
Omaha, NE 68104

Phone: 402-553-1200
Fax: 402-553-0507

email: j1200@aol.com
online catalog: www.centering.org

If reading this book moves you to cry, try to accept this reaction. These are healing tears of grief. They are also tears of health and strength that merge with those of other bereaved parents.

You are not alone.

This book is dedicated to
the parents who shared their experiences for this book;
their babies;
your babies.

Contents

A Note from Debbie

This book is written specifically for bereaved parents who decided to turn away from aggressive medical intervention for their critically ill newborn. The parents featured inside represent a wide variety of situations. Some decided to turn off the ventilator that was breathing for their baby whose brain damage or lung deterioration had diminished chances for a reasonable quality of life and independence from machines. Some parents refused authorization for surgery that may have prolonged life but also prolonged dying. In several cases, the surgeries offered were risky or experimental, without any guarantee that the problems would be solved. Other parents refused treatments that would remedy complications but not solve the baby's underlying, catastrophic problems.

Just twenty-five years ago, the only option for these families would have been to let nature take its course. Nowadays, medical technology can intervene in many of the problems presented by pregnancy, delivery, birth defects, disease and premature birth. For many babies, medicine holds out the possibility of total recovery and normal development. But for others, intervention does not offer such promising outcomes. Sometimes, aggressive treatment saves lives but does not restore wholeness. Indeed, these babies' parents sorted through and agonized over such information and ultimately decided that heroic medicine was not the heroic option. Their courage lay in letting go and allowing nature to work. They chose to let go of a cherished baby because they believed that death was preferable to a life of little awareness, too much pain, too many limitations. The heartbreaking dilemma was to choose between terrible and horrible. Their ongoing challenge is to make peace with their decisions.

This book supplements my book, **Empty Cradle, Broken Heart: Surviving the Death of Your Baby**. *For support in grieving and healing, coping with feelings, affirming your baby, relationships, subsequent pregnancy and raising subsequent children, I invite you to read that resource. This book has its own special missions:*

- *To dispute the illusion that medicine gives us control over life and death;*

- *To offer suggestions for coping with the painful feelings, struggles and challenges of turning away from medical intervention;*

- *To let you know you are not alone, that other parents have made this decision and survived;*

- *To validate the incredible unfairness of such decisions;*

- *To point out the courage and devotion in letting go with love.*

The Triumphs and Traps of Modern Medicine

In the last fifty years, we have seen and benefited from incredible advances in medical knowledge, techniques and therapies. Vaccinations save thousands of children from crippling, fatal diseases. Surgeries reconstruct or even replace vital organs. Drugs fend off ravaging bacteria or restore chemical balance. Modern medicine has enabled us to live healthier, and even longer, lives.

As medicine has helped us fend off many fatal diseases, there has been a shift in how we view death. Many conditions previously considered *terminal* are now considered *treatable*. Death has become something we try to avoid. Rather than being seen as a natural and inevitable part of life, death is perceived as the enemy to be fought at all costs. We share a general fear and denial surrounding death. We don't want to talk about it. We don't want to be around it. We have taken death away from home and family and banished it to hospitals, nursing homes and mortuaries.

This cultural/emotional rejection of death is starting to change, however. In recent years we have begun to reexamine death as a stage of life. Dying and grieving are now considered processes and opportunities for growth; hospices have been established to aid people in these journeys. Included in this movement is a reassessment of how modern medicine fits into our lives and deaths. For instance, living wills allow us to think through and decide how we want our own dying to be managed. Many of us recognize that modern medicine can do more harm than good when all it accomplishes is prolonged suffering with no hope of recovery. Some conditions are terminal, and treatment, other than pain control, can be counterproductive. Instead of surrendering to technology's *do everything possible because it can be done*, we are starting to evaluate how technology can be used in the most humane, compassionate, nurturing and ethically responsible way. We are appreciating that the main goal of medicine should be health, not simply maintenance of life. Medicine fails us when painful or marginal existence is perpetuated. Perhaps there *are* some fates worse than death.

As we learn to embrace death for the end of our lives, we still reject death for those in the bloom of youth. It is difficult to accept the fact that children must sometimes die, and unthinkable that a baby's life, which has hardly begun, must end. And so, the changes occurring in the critical care of the elderly are met with more resistance when applied to the critical care of the young.

The Special Challenges of Neonatal Medicine

It was a really wonderful time in our lives. We couldn't wait for him to be born. We had so many plans . . .

Claudia

The death of a baby shatters our expectations. While we know that people get old and die, we expect babies to have a long life ahead of them. Their bodies should be fresh and new, unspoiled by disease and fast living. Obstetricians and neonatologists are not immune to these expectations and in fact, have chosen a specialty devoted to the beginning of life, not the end. They are committed to using medical technology to ensure that every baby gets the best start. However, some babies have conditions for which modern medicine has no answers or cures. For some, life would be so painful, bleak or meaningless, that the best start can be death.

This is a harsh reality that many people, parents, and professionals, do not want to accept. Indeed, a *survival at all costs* attitude pervades neonatal intensive care medicine and with it, an attempt to skirt the fears and failure associated with the death of a baby. As a result, neonatal medicine tends to focus on the benefits of medical technology but not its limits; medical progress without enough consideration of the risks; the body and body parts instead of the whole child; and the initiation of life support without equal permission to withdraw it. For parents confronted with decisions about aggressive medical intervention, it can be difficult to face these feelings, overcome these biases, and try to find a balanced outlook on what technology can and cannot do for their baby.

You grow up believing doctors can do anything, and even when they take you in a back room and you know something serious is up, it's the farthest thing from your mind that what it is, is your child is going to die.

Wade

I wish someone who had shown me the level 3 nursery had been frank enough to say that not all babies born that early make it. I saw miracles happening and babies smaller than I had ever imagined thriving and going home. I never thought about the cost emotionally or physically or monetarily. That was not what I wanted to see or was allowed to see. So I assumed that even with James' birth defects, that miracles would continue to happen.

                                                                    Grace

The Benefits and Limits of Neonatal Intensive Care

Great strides have been made in the medical treatment of critically ill newborns. Premature babies who would have perished twenty years ago may now be saved by elaborate treatments. Babies whose health is compromised by a difficult pregnancy or delivery can benefit from aggressive intervention. Babies born with birth defects may be restored to health with reconstructive surgery. Babies who would have died from infection or disease may now recover under intensive care. As the *miracles* of modern medicine grab headlines, many parents assume that technology can fix whatever ails their baby. Fortunately, most parents will never have to test this assumption. Unfortunately, for those who do, some discover that neonatal intensive care can't promise a healthy baby.

Every year in the United States, about 250,000 babies are admitted to neonatal intensive care units shortly after birth. Some just need a little jump start, extra special handling to get them on their way. Others face a rocky road full of setbacks and triumphs, but after an initial struggle, grow up healthy and whole. Many other babies aren't so lucky. Treated aggressively in the hope that their uncertain prognosis will turn into recovery and normal development, these babies never thrive. Some cannot overcome the physical or neurological damage resulting from premature birth and aggressive medical interventions. Others with severe birth defects or disease hang on to a marginal, debilitating, even stressful existence. Some of these children spend years in the hospital, hooked up to machines, enduring uncomfortable, often painful *lifesaving* procedures. Some finally go home after a couple of years and, away from emergency interventions, die within a few months.

Even with the dismal outcome for some babies, our culture's widespread distaste for death puts a lot of pressure on medicine to salvage babies for whom nature never intended survival. With blind faith in modern medicine, it is easy to get caught up in rescue fantasies and lose sight of the limits of medical technology. However, it is important to remember that sometimes, refusing medical technology holds the greater benefit.

One of the issues with Johanna was that she could live a natural life that's very short or a totally unnatural life, 100% unnatural, that was an undefined length of time.

Wade

Medical Progress and Risks

As the techniques of diagnosis, oxygen therapies, intravenous nutrition, temperature maintenance, medications and surgeries have improved for premature and sick newborns, the challenge has become application of these therapies in even smaller and sicker infants. The babies who struggle through experimental treatment today will benefit the babies of tomorrow, and herein lies a dilemma. In the seductive world of medical technology and progress, there is not always a rigorous inquiry into the benefits versus harm incurred by aggressive intervention. A very sick baby may be coaxed to survive, but what physical price will this baby pay? What will the quality of this child's life be? Is suffering justified because health will be restored, or is the result merely a painful or marginal existence? Is suffering justified because of its contribution to medical knowledge?

Recognizing the limits and risks of medical technology is a tremendous challenge, especially within a system that may consider it an accomplishment to keep a terminally ill baby alive longer with machines and resuscitation. But NICU staff and parents are starting to reject this blind commitment to heroic intervention and progress which for too many babies has led to prolonged suffering, delayed dying, or survival with severe disabilities.

Parents and health care providers are in a position to weigh the costs and benefits of each medical intervention for each particular baby. When treatment is experimental or prognosis uncertain, parents must decide whether they want their baby to endure the risks and bear the consequences. While outcome can be difficult to predict, the best decisions are based on probability rather than exception, on the burden of the facts rather than a dim ray of hope. Sometimes refusing aggressive medical intervention can be the greater progress.

We were haunted by the possibility that if we chose surgery, Jacob might die without much knowledge of our love for him. He would not have been held for any length of time by us; he just would've known and been cuddled by machines. I felt that if we could hold him and be with him that at least if he died, he would know that we loved him. We thought that it was of paramount importance that he understand what it is to be loved.

Claudia

Treating the Body and Parts in Isolation

Just as it is easy but shortsighted to focus on medical treatment without considering its outcome, it is easy to focus on body parts and lose sight of the body as a whole. Medical specialists tend to be committed to their part of the body and can get caught up in solving the problems presented by the one organ or system of their expertise. So while the lungs are treated, the baby's dying is prolonged, but the doctor can claim *success* because the baby did not die for lack of lung.

Similarly, some doctors don't want to allow a baby to die for lack of technical skill. If they can fix it, they do, sometimes even when the baby is dying from underlying problems. For example, medical care for a baby may include:
• ventilator support to fix breathing
• intravenous nutrition to fix feeding
• antibiotics to fix infection
• surgeries to fix obstructions
• resuscitation to fix cardiac arrest

All so that the baby should die of the problem that cannot be fixed: major organ disintegration. The outcome, death, remains the same, but the route becomes circuitous as medical staff may try to make sure the baby dies of his disease and not from treatable complications which, incidentally could serve to hasten death and reduce a baby's suffering. This aggressive intervention may seem insane, and many parents, as well as health care providers, can be very frustrated by such thinking. The authors of **Mixed Blessings** report seeing a thoughtful sign in a doctor's office: *If God gives you an infant but takes away the lungs, heart, kidneys, or brain, maybe He's trying to tell you something.*

A more complex but more humane approach takes into account the whole child. A holistic evaluation of aggressive treatment considers the emotional, physical, intellectual and social consequences for the baby, not just for the body or body part. A holistic evaluation also takes a hard look at the consequences for the family, as it is the family who will carry the responsibility of the child's care and development. Smart, sensitive parents appreciate the enormous burdens of caring for a chronically ill, severely disabled, or unresponsive child and want to know about the long-term impact. If this responsibility will lead to the disintegration of the family and its members, then no one's needs are best served.

Even if a family is emotionally and financially well-equipped to handle such a child, the cost is still humanly excessive.

It is not fair to the baby to salvage a life full of pain and debilitation, doomed to neglect or resentment by exhausted parents or sentenced to custodial institutional care. The challenge for parents and doctors is to look at the big picture and determine what is in the baby's best interest, not just what's best for a particular organ or the body. Death can be an important option to consider. Death is a part of life, sad, often tragic, but a natural and sometimes preferable path.

Birth defects. That's what James had. Defects. Born with them. And one alone might have been okay but multiple meant compounded problems and maybe not able to be solved with a little tuck here and a little surgery there. Although I never got a definitive answer from any of the specialists, I kept asking, what would life hold for James? Would any of these doctors be proud to say, "Yes, sir, that's MY baby!"

Grace

I've radically changed my thinking of saving a life at all costs. I feel there are times when the technology goes too far, and we the parents (not the doctors) have to endure the consequences. Quality of life needs to count more than it does!

Beth

The Dilemmas of Withdrawing Mechanical Life Support

When we were told all brain wave activity had stopped, termination was discussed. Someone said he could live indefinitely in the state he was in so I think our choices were basically allowing his body to die or let it live with the use of machines. Mark would never be anything, but, as my husband said, a vegetable.

Beth

While withdrawing mechanical life support can unquestionably be the best thing for the baby, it is still an agonizing process. When death is held at bay by technology, someone must be responsible for recognizing when to allow death to come. For parents, this decision is heart-wrenching because it is the final defeat against their desire to have this baby come home, to live and grow up. For medical professionals, this decision goes against the grain of their focus on saving lives. Doctors vary on where they draw the line. Some see themselves as an unyielding foe of death, a value firmly ingrained in our culture. They ask, *What gives us the right to play God and discontinue life support?* Others see that death is an unyielding part of life. More to the point, they ask, *What gives us the right to play God and continue life support?*

Sometimes, reluctance to remove life support comes from fear. It seems scary being around a dying baby and it is daunting to feel responsible for letting death come. For health care providers, even if death is inevitable, some see it as a failure. There is also a competitive urge to cheat death. A prevailing mentality among some medical staff is, *No one is going to die on my shift.*

Other times, reluctance to remove life support comes from the huge investment of effort and resources devoted to keeping a baby alive. To pull the plug *after all we've been through* seems like such a waste. To pull the plug is admitting that *we were wrong about this baby's prognosis.* To pull the plug can seem like abandoning a baby who has *put up such a valiant fight.* Instead, it is easier to put it off, like throwing good money after bad in the vain hope of recouping the losses or justifying the investment. It can be difficult to know when enough is enough.

The Fallacies of "Miracle Babies"

Miracle babies sometimes occur because of a misdiagnosis. When a severe heart defect corrects itself, then apparently the heart defect was misdiagnosed and proved to be less severe than the doctors originally thought. When *hopelessly abnormal* brain activity becomes normal, apparently the brain activity was not *hopelessly abnormal* after all. When *irreparably damaged* lungs become capable of taking air, obviously those lungs were not *irreparably damaged.* If your baby's dismal diagnosis was mistaken, then your baby would have also shown "miraculous improvement."

Other babies become miracles because they beat the odds. They survived risky surgery, did not reject a transplanted organ, or the experimental therapy worked for them. Just the fact that doctors call these babies miracles is a testament to how amazing it is that they did so well. And chances are, the details of their situation were different from your baby's. For whatever reason, the "miracle baby" stood a better chance. Under better circumstances, you might have reached for a miracle. But you had the sense to make your decision based on risks, probabilities and the burden of the facts presented to you, not based on fantasy and wishful thinking.

More About Some of Those "Miracle Babies". . .

The stories we hear about miracle babies usually boast about their survival against great odds. A baby born extremely prematurely is now babbling and playing. A baby with a transplanted organ is toddling about. A baby with spinal deformities is now sitting up with support. A baby with chromosomal abnormalities can smile. What we often don't hear about is what it took to get there, what it's really like, and what is required for continued survival.

The baby born so premature that she was unlikely to survive – she spent her first eight months of life in the hospital, enduring needles, tubes, infections, suctioning, drugs and surgeries. Her eyesight was so damaged by oxygen therapies that she is considered legally blind. She still requires oxygen through a nose cannula, has cerebral palsy and requires frequent intravenous nutrition because of feeding and digestion problems. Her development is delayed and she will continue to need therapies, special schooling and life-long custodial care.

The baby born with the need for an organ transplant spent the first year of his life in and out of hospitals until a donor was found. In all that time he was so sick he never learned to sit up or play with toys and his development continues to lag. The risky surgery was followed by a long and painful recuperation. He will need to stay on immuno-suppressant drugs that may prevent him from rejecting the foreign organ, but the same drugs also result in growth retardation and frequent bouts with serious illnesses. He will always be at risk of needing anther transplant and must refrain from many activities his peers can enjoy.

The baby with the severe spinal deformities was not expected to survive – she endured five separate surgeries before she was a year old. She was traumatized by the prolonged hospitalization and separations and has not developed a healthy emotional attachment to her parents. She screams at the sight of any health professional. She faces more surgeries and will never walk, control her bladder or bowels, and constant bladder infections will ultimately lead to kidney damage and biweekly dialysis.

The baby with the chromosomal abnormality was aggressively resuscitated at birth and placed on a ventilator and intravenous feedings to make up for her poor lung and digestive function. She was given medication to control the seizures in her malformed brain. While she is now breathing on her own, she will always be bedridden, medicated, fed through a gastrostomy tube, and minimally responsive to her environment.

That these children survived against great odds is true. But when you get more information, these "miracles" dissolve into incredible struggles and suffering. In fact, each of these children could still die from complications of chronic conditions before reaching a third birthday. There are those who would call that a blessing.

It can help to remember that your baby would have paid a high price in terms of pain and suffering in any quest for a miracle. Even the promise of a long, fairly normal life may not cancel this price. For instance, the parents of Isabelle, the miracle baby born at twenty-three weeks who came home after six months of hospitalization and countless needles, procedures and surgeries, have a plan for what they will do if faced with another twenty-three week premature birth. They will drive to a small, unsophisticated hospital and let nature take its course.

In the crib next to James for a few days was a baby girl, just a year old. This child had tubes and a respirator and all sorts of things going into and out of her body. Her mother was in taking care of her one day and we talked a little. Her daughter, it turned out, had some of the same problems as James and had survived an infection or two. She had celebrated her first birthday in the hospital and there were remnants of the celebration around her bed. Vinyl balloons, cards, scraps of wrapping paper, new clothes. But this little girl could barely see. She could barely move on her own. She couldn't sit by herself, eat by herself, play by herself, or any of the "normal" things I remember my 11 year old doing at one year. This little girl was severely retarded, had seizures, and it did not appear that she would ever "know" anything. I had to look at her and imagine James that way in a year. Would I ever want to visit a child like that? Could that child ever know I was visiting? Could I ever forget that I had had a normal child and not compare James' accomplishments to my daughter's? Could I celebrate the fact that James' biggest feat of the month might be taking 4 ounces of formula by mouth and not by a tube? Could I ever look at James and not think what I thought each day when I saw that little girl? What is the point of this life? What will this person, who deserves respect and care and love, ever know? Who decided that this little girl deserved to live a life of laying in a bed on her back unaware of the world around her, unaware of her own body? What was there to be gained by these decisions?

Grace

Parents who turn away from aggressive medical intervention for their infants are sometimes scorned in this age of high technology and incredible advances. There is a lot of social pressure to *go for it* and use the best technology that medicine offers. If the baby survives and thrives, she is labeled a miracle, and the family appears on television shows and in the popular magazines. People feel inspired by their tenacity in the face of great odds.

As a result of this public admiration, parents who choose nonintervention can feel put on the defensive, even though by some standards, theirs was the more heroic decision. Indeed, it is much harder to let go than to hold on. These are the parents who have the courage to let go and meet death, with tears and clenched fists, but on some level accepting what is inevitable for all of us.

We didn't want to let go of this baby. We just got him, we just met him, we just found out how much we love him. We don't want to let go. But to be good parents, to look after his needs, maybe this is what's best for him.

Claudia

Facing the Decision

The pediatrician sort of fell on his knees beside the bed and put his arm across me and said, "I have some terrible news, your baby has a terrible problem and it's so terrible we don't expect him to live." I think a part of me is back there still.

Claudia

Most parents slip into shock and denial when first informed that their baby is critically ill. Although you can hear the doctors reporting some very bad news, a part of you holds onto the hope that there has been a mistake or that there is a way to fix everything. Sometimes reality sinks in when the doctors talk straightforwardly about severe handicaps or probable death. Sometimes reality sinks in when you see the baby full of tubes and wires. In any case, feelings of shock can linger even after your baby dies.

I knew when he was born he had very little chance for survival. He was so little, and I was so frightened. I had never seen a baby so tiny. Intellectually I thought he wouldn't survive. My heart hoped and prayed that he would.

Lena

It is overwhelming to be faced with making such important decisions when you're just fighting to grasp reality. If you are also recovering from anesthesia, drugged for pain, or simply exhausted, wading through all the technical terms and information can feel like an insurmountable task.

Gathering Information

There are so many questions to ask: Questions about diagnoses, treatments, logistics, outcomes and prognoses. Since many decisions must be reached in a matter of days, even hours, you may have only wanted to deal with medical information and statistics pertaining specifically to your baby's condition. Often there is no time or emotional energy to deal with anything else.

Although the questions can seem endless, even more overwhelming is the fact that many may not have answers. One of the most aggravating aspects of gathering information is that so much of it is in the form of educated guesses, divergent opinions, approximations, contingencies and statistics. None of these could tell you exactly what would happen with your baby. Nevertheless, you had to rely on what information you could get. As Molly points out, *We wanted as many opinions as possible about the various options from specialists.* Lena agrees. *What I needed and got from my doctor were facts and educated guesses on Stephen's possible future health. I relied on his experience in the medical field.*

Unfortunately, communication with the doctors can be hampered during a crisis. A common dynamic is when the doctor focuses on physiological issues to the exclusion of emotional ones; meanwhile you are in acute emotional shock and tune out much of the medical information presented. That's why it can help to go over information more than once, preferably in written form or audio tapes of your meetings.

Another frustration is the sheer volume of information you may have felt was critical to making an informed decision. Receiving a crash course in human physiology and pathology with all the unfamiliar terminology can be mind boggling. Add all the different indicators, alternatives, and consequences, and it can be a monumental struggle to sort through and stay on top of the situation.

The following lists of questions were gathered from a number of parents who faced different situations. Remember, even if you had been able to pose every one, the definitive answers would have been few and far between. But by reviewing them, you may clarify or even find new support for your decision.

The most pressing questions likely involved trying to understand your baby's problems and treatment options.

- What is the medical explanation of my baby's condition?
- What does my baby's condition look like compared to "normal"?
- What are the theories on the cause of my baby's condition?
- How often does this happen?
- What is the chance of misdiagnosis?
- What are our options?

- What are the actual treatments or surgical procedures?
- How exactly are they done?
- What are their chances of success with my baby?
- What are the survival rates, short-term and long-term?
- Where are they performed (nearby hospital or miles away)?
- Does the family have to relocate?
- Who would be performing treatments or surgery?
- What are this doctor's experiences and success rate?
- What do the treatments or surgeries cost?
- How long will my baby need to undergo this treatment?
- What are the risks of this treatment?
- What are the side effects of this treatment?
- What are the logistics of carrying out this treatment?
- Will mechanical life support be necessary?
- What kinds of mechanical life support?
- Can we withdraw life support once it has begun?
- How likely is it that a suitable donor organ will be found?
- How long must my baby wait before surgery can be performed?
- Can anything else be done?
- Do I have the legal right to make this decision?
- What if close family members strongly disagree with our decision?

You may have had many questions about short-term and long-term quality of life.

- Is it reasonable to try to repair, replace, or live with this condition?
- What will my baby's life be like while waiting for surgery?
- What will my baby's life be like while in the intensive care unit?
- What kind of recovery (full/partial/minimal) is likely to occur?
- How long would recovery take?
- What is the recovery process like?
- What problems cannot be fixed?
- How much pain is endured?
- What medications are necessary?
- What are the side effects of medications?
- What follow-up procedures are necessary?
- Will more surgeries be needed?
- How much of my child's life is likely to be spent in the hospital?
- What will life be like for my baby during treatment?
- What will life be like afterward?

- Will there be continued threats to my child's health?
- Will intellectual, physical or emotional development be impaired?
- Will my child be able to participate fully in normal activities?
- Will my child grow normally?
- How long do children with this condition live?
- If treatments are initially successful, what are the chances of my baby dying later during childhood?

There may have been broader family issues to sort out.

- Will my child be able to live at home?
- What impact will this have on our marriage?
- What impact will this have on our other children?
- What impact will this have on our future children?
- What impact will this have on our finances?
- What emotional impact will this have on me?
- Are there support services available to help me with my child's care?
- Do we have the support of close family members?
- What about relinquishing my child to an institution, a foster home or adoption?

You may have wanted to know how other parents feel about their decision to let go.

- How do they feel about their decision 1 month, 1 year, 5 years later?
- Did they want to leave the hospital and let nature take its course?
- How do parents who took their baby home to die feel about this option?
- In hindsight, are there certain things they're glad they did, or things they wish they had done?
- When death is near, what are some of the things that other parents have found helpful to do?

You may have had more questions about death and dying.

- What would it be like to take my baby home and have her or him die there?
- What would it be like to watch my baby die? Would it be scary?
- What does the dying process look like? What can I expect?
- What are the signs of death being near?

- Will my baby be in pain? Do babies feel themselves dying?
- What can be done to make my baby most comfortable?
- Is there hospice care available in my area?
- What can I do when I'm second-guessing myself and my decision?

There are also questions you may not have wanted to ask. You probably didn't want to hear diatribes on generic or abstract ideas about quality of life or medical technology. You especially may not have wanted information about bereavement and grief. Claudia found this to be the case for her and John. She explains, *The child's lifetime is not the time to raise the specter of grief. It is the time for parents to be focused on their child as he or she is. While we were in the hospital with Jacob, a woman who had lost her firstborn to hypoplastic left heart syndrome was also in the hospital delivering her third child. She paid us a visit and spoke a great deal about her family's grieving process. This was not helpful to us at the time, and we sat there wishing she would leave. A phone call after death would have been better!*

Molly elaborates: *I can remember a few things I didn't care about while Peter was alive, although I wanted the information after he died – like support groups – because we were praying for a miracle and hadn't accepted the fact that Peter was really going to die. Or how to talk to siblings about the situation – we were too focused on Peter to even remember we had two other children! And ethics/morality of the decision – this was something we had to search our hearts for without others' opinions.*

You may have discovered that you came into this situation with some basic philosophies about life and death, however instinctive or thought out, tentative or sure. The decisions for your baby brought them to the fore, making you clarify your values and apply them. As Claudia points out, applying these values is not so easy: *We were fortunate in that we had already discussed our basic philosophies concerning heroic medicine prior to Jacob's birth. But it's one thing to discuss heroic medicine around the table and say, "I don't think I'd subject my child to that," and it's another thing to actually have that child. Then you have to face choices where every option is terrible.*

Here are some of the broader medical/social issues which may have helped you clarify your values and decisions.

- Is it really heroic to keep a terminally ill baby alive longer than expected with medical technology?
- Is it realistic or desirable to try to salvage every life?
- Should the benefits of medical technology be measured by the number of lives saved, or by the quality of lives saved?
- Is medical progress a goal that justifies the means?
- Is it always a realistic or desirable goal to thwart death?
- Would health dollars be better spent on preventative prenatal and pediatric care (to which many cannot afford access) rather than on emergency and intensive care which wage far more costly battles?
- Can society truly accommodate my disabled child with educational, vocational, or custodial care programs?
- Will society support our family with financial, emotional, and medical resources if we take on this child's care?

While these are global and abstract questions, you faced them in your own life, with your own baby. Even as you balance the rational social arguments, turning away from aggressive medical intervention is still a very personal, emotional and heart-wrenchingly difficult decision.

We weighed so many factors as we made our final decision about Jacob's future. But I believe that both of us had already made our decision by the time the doctors finished explaining the situation to us. Though all of the facts and logistics were important, what guided us most was an innate, gut-level sense that human beings are not machines, that our body parts are not indiscriminately interchangeable, that our society spends too much of its resources in flight from death, and that there are times when death, no matter how painful it may be, how unnatural it may seem, must simply be met. We felt that a heart incapable of functioning was one of those cases.

Claudia

Your religious beliefs may have also played an important role in helping you consider letting nature take its course. Beth remembers, *With a wonderful hospital chaplain, we came to the conclusion that Mark had really already died; his soul had gone to heaven and his body was simply kept alive by machines.*

You may even start to question whether medical treatment is actually interfering with your child's destiny. Kristin remembers, *As another intervention took place, I began to wonder if we had already tampered with God's plan for Jenna. This realization made it possible to say "No" to further interventions.*

You may have also gotten a sense of permission for letting go. Hannah recalls, *My religious background and our pastor were supportive in offering the perspective that God cares in all situations, even when it means letting go. I did not feel God would condemn us for not trying longer.*

Lena agrees, *It was important to me to be assured that "pulling the plug" would be OK in God's eyes. Even so, letting Stephen go for it on his own without artificial help was probably the hardest decision I have faced or ever will face.*

Making the Decision

Even with every possible shred of information at hand and values thought out, making the final decision can be extremely difficult for a number of reasons:

- Uncertainties inherent in the medical treatments and prognosis
- The pressure of time constraints
- The gravity and irreversibility of the decision
- The challenge of figuring out what is in the baby's best interest
- The roller coaster ride of intense emotions
- The hard task of facing death

The Uncertainties

Ambiguities make decisions difficult. When a baby's condition is complex, the diagnosis mysterious, the prognosis uncertain or the treatment risky, then the best course is unclear. Sometimes it is impossible to predict which infants will thrive, which ones will merely survive, and which ones will die even after maximum intervention.

One of the issues with Joanna was they could not reassure us that there was even a good chance, even a 50/50 chance she would even make it through surgery. They couldn't even give us hope of that.

Wade

Another aspect of uncertainty is when the proposed treatments are experimental. As the frontier of medical knowledge moves onward, infants who would have merely survived a few years ago can be offered a good chance to thrive. Some of what was unknown twenty years ago is now familiar territory. However, pushing the frontier will always include the process of discovering therapies that work well and discarding ones that prove not to. The question for individual families becomes, *Do we give our baby to medical science and say, "OK, experiment on this child?"* In addition, research statistics are almost useless when you are trying to weigh the risks and benefits of treatment for your individual child. It's impossible to answer the question, *Will my baby be one of the several out of 10 (or 100, or 1,000) who will benefit from this treatment?*

More uncertainties arise with conflicting opinions among doctors. One specialist may feel strongly that intervention is the way to go and another may feel quite the opposite. When you're making a decision, conflicting opinions can be confusing and disturbing. If an ethics committee is brought in or legal action is threatened, you suffer additional agony over your decision and fear losing the ability to pursue what you believe to be the best interests of your own child. Faced with this possibility, Grace says, *It was unsettling to think that even if I believed in letting nature take its course, the medical ethics committee could overrule that decision and do extraordinary things to James if they felt his life was worth saving.*

Finally, the whole issue of quality of life is ambiguous. There is no consensus on what exactly constitutes an acceptable quality of life, no total agreement on where to draw the line. The more dismal the quality of life, the less consensus there is. However, most people agree that the two extreme positions – preserve life no matter what versus preserve only life of highest quality – are foolish. Reasonable decisions demand delicate judgments, and there is no absolute right or wrong between the extremes.

Given all the uncertainties and ambiguities, at some point you had to choose which guesses, opinions and statistics to rely on. You had to decide how to balance possible risks against probable outcome. With regard to quality of life, you had to decide for yourself, and your baby, where to draw the line. While your decisions may have felt like shots in the dark, you did the best you could with imperfect information.

Time Constraints

Our decision-making time was extremely intense. We felt pressed to arrive at a decision quickly because the doctors didn't feel that Jacob was going to live very long without drastic intervention. If we were to pursue surgery, we needed to get him on life support as quickly as possible and initiate a search for a heart, or get him to Philadelphia for the Norwood procedure. If we were to allow nature to take its course, we needed to remove the tubes and needles so that he could be as comfortable as possible for as long as possible, and we needed to get to him, to be with him for as long as we could.

Claudia

With so much information to digest and so many emotions to sort through, time constraints can increase the stress of the decision-making process. If you had this additional pressure, you may have felt more confused about the options and more uncertain about your choice. You may have wanted more time to collect information and deliberately comb through it. You may have wished you had time to regain some emotional equilibrium.

Having additional time may have helped you feel more sure and perhaps let you come to a comfortable consensus with your partner before making the final decisions. Even so, whether you had two seconds or two years, you most likely would have come to the same conclusions. And even if you had two years, the emotional turmoil would still accompany your decision. Indeed, the decision-making process doesn't end with a decision. It is afterward that eventually most of your stress fades, your confidence grows and you and your partner can come together. As you grieve, your second-guessing wanes; you adjust and find peace. There is no deadline for the post-decision part of the process.

Another stress imposed by time constraints is wishing you could have spent more time with your baby. In hindsight, you may wonder why you didn't do more things like kissing and cuddling. It is important to remember that even when parents feel like they spent a lot of time with their baby, they may always wish they could have had more time, a lifetime. Your sadness and regrets about this are an integral and natural part of your grieving process.

I went to see Stephen. He had so many tubes and gadgets. I was afraid to pick him up and hold him. So I hugged him while he lay there in the isolette. If I had it to do again, I would pick him up, hold him, hug him, rock him, talk to him and sing to him.

Lena

After an emergency C-section, I was getting pain medications that literally knocked me out. Also, not being in the same hospital as Laura, I didn't see her much. But the NICU staff would call me periodically to ask if I had questions and to tell me that Gene was with Laura. He held her almost half the time she was alive. They let him hold her while they did procedures, and he remembers feeling that she seemed less agitated when he held her. That really meant a lot to me. I really wanted to be with her. *

Hannah

The Gravity of the Decision

Most of us find it easy to make a decision when it's routine or easily changed and when the consequences are fleeting or minor. But when a decision is extraordinary, we can't rely on past experience to guide us. When a decision is irreversible or the consequences permanent, we hesitate to make our final stand. There are no second chances. When the consequences are life-changing, we want to be certain we make the right decision, the best choice. When all of the alternatives are terrible, it is doubly hard to figure out what is best.

Your decision about aggressive medical intervention has all of these characteristics. On top of everything, you may feel you really don't want the responsibility of making such a grave and irrevocable decision. As Beth points out, *The hardest part in making this decision was the feeling that we were asked to play God. It seemed that we had just given this child life, and they were asking us to take it away from him.*

The Best Interests of the Child

So much we wanted him with us, we wanted him to grow with us at all costs. Part of me is saying "at all costs" but the rational part of me is saying, "but what about how he feels?"

Molly

Most parents agree that the critical factor in their decision was the thier baby's welfare. The best choice became what they believed was best for their child.

In addition to considering quality of life, many parents try to determine what the child would have chosen. This can be especially challenging to do for a baby because there are no living wills or discussions about quality of life and heroic medicine. With an older child or adult, simply having known the person can offer a sense of what she or he would have wanted. You could consider things like, *She wouldn't have wanted to be trapped inside a body rendered useless by disease – she so loved sports,* or *He wouldn't have wished to live in a vegetative state, his mind was so bright and curious.* Nevertheless, you can assume your child would have wanted to be whole and healthy, with the potential to develop a love of activity and learning. From that wish, you could infer what she or he might have wanted.

One pediatric surgeon asked us this question: If Jenna could have clarity of thought, and was able to look down on her condition, seeing all that existed, would she want to continue? My husband and I both answered instantaneously, "No!" In our case, seeing how poorly our daughter developed and how much she struggled every minute of every day brought us to our decision more than any other reason.

Kristin

Rightly so, determining your baby's best interests depended on your values and projections. As Claudia points out, *We did not feel that the life of pain and uncertainty offered by the surgeries was one that we would choose for ourselves, and we did not feel comfortable choosing such a life for Jacob.*

I had to think what was best for him. I firmly believe he would have fought for his life if that is what I wanted, but was that the best for him? Was forcing life on a body that was so incomplete the best I could do for him? I wanted him to be happy and free. I had to prepare myself to let him go. And I had to let him know that I loved him and I wanted so much more for him because of who he was. He was a kind, peaceful person who gave peace to all who knew him. I didn't want him to lead a long, unpeaceful life of struggle. I couldn't ask that of one so small. The best I could do was to let go. The hardest thing I could do was to let go.

Grace

The Roller Coaster of Emotions

Facing and coming to a decision is often described as a roller coaster of intense emotions. The ups and downs can be swift and unpredictable. Grace describes those days.

The whole decision-making process was a roller coaster of intensely good and hellishly awful feelings, doubts and fears. It was a runaway train of thoughts and days of time going too slowly sometimes, too quickly when I wasn't prepared for it. It was hours, days of imagining what life would be like for James, struggling to remember simple things like sucking. It was hours, days of fearing what life would be like for me – my son in the care of strangers because I didn't have the medical sophistication necessary to care for my own flesh and blood. It was days and hours of saying good-bye forever to a baby I loved who would never be. It was willing James to live, fearing he would die; fearing he would live, willing him to die. It was days, weeks of looking for answers only to be met with more questions and uncertainties.

Grace

While the roller coaster ride can be unbearable, it does start to smooth out once a final decision is made. Some parents recall that moment, when their decision crystallized and they knew it was right. For Ted, it was when the doctor pointed out, *There are some fates worse than death.* Molly agrees: *I remember walking into the intensive care unit where they put him on monitors until we made our decision and seeing him all hooked up; I knew I couldn't do that to him.* Beth recalls a couple of key moments: *Our own pastor said he felt God would bless our decision, and that's when I knew the decision was right. The first time I held Mark was shortly after we made this decision and again, I knew it was right.*

When Jenna became unable to suck/ swallow, I knew we were all faced with a life-changing decision. This happened from one feeding to the next. I remember releasing long, sorrowful low tones as I cried... Sometimes, (declining intervention) is simply the "next step".

Kristin

Facing Death

Some babies die before or very soon after treatment is discontinued or refused. For many parents, this is strong and reassuring evidence that they made the right choice. Other babies may live for several hours, days or even months before they die. These parents may be alternately grateful for the time they have with their baby and agonized over watching their baby die. Every day is precious, yet the lingering and uncertainty of when death will come can be unnerving. It can be an extraordinary, bittersweet time.

It's so hard to hold your baby in your arms knowing you've chosen not to do everything possible to save his life. I will never forget that feeling.

Beth

Peter spoke to us in volumes in eight days. He was loved for eight entire days. There is a part of him that will always be a part of me. For the rest of my life, it's prioritized. He did that.

Ted

Many parents say that nurturing their baby is an important way to cope with the fact that death is imminent. Nursing, feeding, bathing, dressing, holding your baby skin-to-skin, and just spending time with your little one gives you opportunities to demonstrate your love, to be parents, and let your baby know what it is to be loved. Courtney says, *For eight days, I was never too tired. I didn't sleep; I didn't eat. She got everything we had, everything.* This time with your baby can also create memories that will later help you with the grieving process.

After they took her off the respirator, we were alone with her, holding her, talking to her, really trying to let go, to say good-bye. We had those moments with her – she knows and I know. That's the most rewarding part of it all. We were able to say hello and say our good-byes. I feel blessed that we had her for those moments. That's what got me through it, the hellos and good-byes.

Rita

You will also benefit from collecting keepsakes such as locks of hair, plaster or ink footprints and handprints, blankets and outfits your baby wore, and photographs, including a family portrait, and pictures of you holding your baby close. The objects you collect and create are tangible things you can see, touch and hold. As you grieve, having these keepsakes can help you hold onto your memories and feel close to your baby.

Unfortunately, not every parent has the opportunity or the encouragement to spend time with their baby or to collect many keepsakes. Hannah spoke earlier about how a Cesarean delivery, pain medications, and separate hospitals made it impossible for her to spend much time with Laura. Rachel has similar regrets. These too must be grieved.

Making plans for my child's upcoming death is a notion I would have embraced if it had only occurred to me during the frenzy of our son's short life. I never realized having the baby near me 24 hours a day, getting the opportunity to bathe and feed him, and certainly arranging to be with him when he died could be important later on. Only after did I learn I could have taken more control over these sorts of details.

Rachel

Every Situation Is Unique

Most parents agree with Ted, *I never made a more difficult decision and I probably never will.* Tragically, for Courtney and Wade, they gave birth to a second baby with another life-threatening condition. But while Johanna's diagnosis had a name but no cure, Preston's diagnosis was a mystery and they were given hope for a cure. Courtney explains, *We thought with Johanna, it would be the hardest decision we'd ever have to make, that all decisions would be easy from here on out. And for a while they were. But then we're faced with decisions about Preston's care and they are not easy, they are just as hard. But the difference between the decisions was that the decisions we made for Preston's were for a cure.*

Wade continues, *Even though Preston has had surgery twice, we've known that going into it, even though he's not going to look too great when he comes out, he is going to come out of surgery. With Johanna, we didn't even know that.*

As Courtney and Wade have discovered, there is no formula for making decisions about aggressive medical intervention. Every baby presents a unique profile, and after gathering as much information as you can about options and prognoses, after weighing the risks and benefits for your baby, after looking into your heart, you just do the best you can.

Is there anything that could've made your decisions easier? Perhaps knowing that other parents had faced similar decisions, perhaps having others help gather information, perhaps being able to spend more time with your baby. But ultimately, most parents believe that there was nothing that would have eased their heartache.

Notes. . .

Making Peace With Your Decision

Besides the painful feelings involved in the grieving process, parents who have made difficult life and death decisions for their babies face the special challenge of coping with worries and doubts about their choices. Did we make the best decision? Is this what our baby wanted? Working through these feelings is a normal, healthy part of grieving. As you come to terms with your baby's death, you will also resolve your worries and doubts.

The following worries and doubts are shared by many bereaved parents who turned away from aggressive intervention.

Did I miss some critical information or advice?

After any difficult, life-changing decision, it is natural to go over and over the facts and retrace your steps. You may wonder if you gathered all the pertinent information, overturned every stone. You may wonder if there were other choices to consider. You may wish you could've talked more with your clergy person or other trusted advisors. But the bottom line is, given the choices, information, resources and time available, you made the best decision possible. It is important to remember that your choices were rightly based on what you could see, hear, or know, not on what was invisible or unattainable.

Should I have trusted the doctor's advice to turn down medical intervention?

Your doctor had the benefit of years of training, experience, collecting and reviewing information, consulting with colleagues and specialists. Chances are, your doctor was better informed than you could ever have hoped to become during your baby's short life. Especially when there are many uncertainties, relying on your doctor's judgment can be the most reasonable course to take. If you discover a few years later that your doctor is giving different advice or is using new techniques, it's because certain things are possible now that were impossible or experimental in your baby's time.

Did my baby feel rejected?

To feel rejected, your baby would have to hold you responsible for death. Besides the fact that infants are incapable of placing blame, you did not abandon your baby to death. You allowed your baby to find his own way. What the baby did sense was your devotion and nurturing. Some parents take comfort in the belief that now their baby is in an all-knowing state and understands their letting go as an act of love.

I was under so much stress. Did that interfere with my judgment?

Many parents worry about making such important decisions under so much duress. However, these kinds of decisions cannot be totally rational. There is a huge and crucial emotional component to the situation. Your emotional duress actually played an important role in your judgment. It enabled you to make the decision with your heart and gut, not just your mind.

But what if we'd continued treatment and to everyone's surprise, the baby thrived?

You can torture yourself with such thoughts, but recognize that this punishes you for declining something that in all likelihood would not have happened anyway. If you could look in a crystal ball and see that your baby would have died or been in a painful or vegetative state no matter what was done, you'd let yourself off the hook. But since you have no crystal ball, you can only make certain assumptions AND **you can choose which assumptions to make:** Ones that let you live in peace, or ones that torture you. Whatever assumption you make doesn't change the outcome or affect your baby. It affects only you and your quality of life. Give yourself permission to accept your decisions as best for your baby.

Did I do what my baby would have wanted?

Many parents are haunted by this question. It is natural for you to be concerned about your baby's own desires. Without absolute confirmation, you may feel unsure about whether your decision was in line with your baby's preferences and destiny. Remember though, you were in an excellent position for making such a judgment. You are closest to your baby in blood, body and spirit. You may feel like you were merely making your best guess, but your best guess is the best one of all. No one else could have done this for your baby as carefully, thoughtfully, purposefully and solemnly as you did. No one else could have been more agonized, calculating and soul-searching. Your decisions were best for your baby. And for a different baby, you might have made different decisions. Trust in your sense of what *this* baby wanted.

What about the ethics of my decision?

A decision is ethical whenever it is based on reasoned argument or valid principles. To make this decision, on some level you engaged in complex ethical thinking. You drew on your basic values of life and death; you weighed costs and benefits and you strove to determine *best interest* and *higher good*. You also came to some of the same conclusions that respected and renowned ethicists have spent years honing. Entire books are written about quality of life, death with dignity, and technology's false conquering of death.

The torment you feel is evidence that you wrestled with complex issues. You were conscientious and reasonable, not glib or simplistic. Your decision was ethical.

It's such a burden to bear. Shouldn't someone else have made the difficult decisions?

You may wish someone else could have made the decisions, someone who knew more, who could think more clearly, who could foresee the future. However, there is no such person. Because these decisions deal heavily in matters of the heart, parents are the most appropriate decision makers. It is a heavy responsibility to bear, but your baby would want you, not strangers, to decide. Indeed, if you had been barred from making these decisions, you would probably feel even more angry and depressed. If it comforts you, you can also remind yourself that you did not decide to let your baby die. You decided to let nature take its course, or to let God's Will be done. Remember the sign on that doctor's wall? *If God gives you an infant but takes away the lungs, heart, kidneys, or brain, maybe He's trying to tell you something.* Your baby had a body that could not thrive outside the womb. Ultimately, that was out of your control.

Will second thoughts always haunt me? How can I stop questioning my decisions?

Asking *what ifs* is a natural part of grief. At first, *what ifs* can be sharp and self-incriminating, but they do not mean you made any wrong decisions. As you work through your grief, particularly your anger and guilt, and as you come to terms with your baby's life and death, you will notice a subtle shift. You will come to accept reality – it happened, that was your decision, you can live with it – instead of wishing things were different. Lingering *what ifs* become reflective, reminiscent, a fantasy to daydream rather than willing reality to change. They may become gentler and broader: *If only he hadn't been born so prematurely*, rather than, *If only we had made different choices*. In time you will be able to let go of what might have been. As your grief diminishes, so will second thoughts.

Your second thoughts may also diminish as you see that in reality, the situation was beyond your control. You did not choose your baby's condition or outcome. Death happened because there were no better possible options. As Hannah points out, *Any second thoughts I had regarding withdrawing life support were brief and probably due to depression, because medically there wasn't anything more that could be done.*

Wrestling with second thoughts can also be a way for you to evaluate, solidify and embrace the beliefs and principles which guided your decision. Claudia read about another family who chose aggressive medical intervention for their baby's heart defect. At first she felt unsettled by doubts. Maybe she should have fought off death, too. But she was also struck by something else. The other mother's worst fear was that her baby would die in her arms. In contrast, Claudia's worst fear was that her baby would *not* die in her arms. These two images beautifully sum up each mother's attitude toward death and the resulting very different decisions.

As you grieve, there may be times when you feel convinced you made some wrong choices. But remember, the alternatives were equally or even more grim, not better for your baby. If only you had decided differently . . . you'd probably feel even worse. So would your baby. Also remember that you feel bad, not because you made bad decisions but because these were painful decisions to make.

The medical staff felt we made the ONLY decision, but I will always wonder. I've seen talk shows where they have children born with Mark's problems and as serious as Mark's who have lived even though severely handicapped. These things make me second guess myself. Someone once told me that death isn't always the worst scenario, and I have to believe that in Mark's life, death was the best alternative. This was the hardest decision I've ever had to make, but I'm sure I would do it again.
                                                                    Beth

Exploring the "road not taken" can be healthy, even necessary. Much of my own healing has come from learning of families who chose aggressive alternatives. I see our philosophical differences and this has become a source of comfort. Their feelings about "life at all costs" are not right for me; my "do nothing" choice unthinkable to them. And we are both right. . .as far as I'm concerned there are no right or wrong answers. Each family must determine what is right for them.

Rachel

Coping With Harsh Judgment

There was one instance where someone felt we had "murdered" our son and that hurt. This person had never walked in my shoes. Even though every other person felt we were courageous and right to do what we did, this one instance stays with me. . .the one comment I can't forget.

Beth

Unfortunately, there are plenty of self-righteous, moralizing people who presume to know what's best for everyone else. Those who oppose your decision may be driven by a naive passion for simplicity. Unable to balance costs and benefits, weigh extenuating circumstances or value the uniqueness of every situation, they cling to a black and white view that life is good and death is bad. There are others whose capacity to reason shuts down when they hear the word "baby." They use simplistic thinking in the form of over generalization; the root of their intolerance is fear. They fear that if we "allow" sick babies to die, next thing you know, we'll be putting pillows over the faces of healthy babies. Despite the obvious differences, they fail to trust the distinction between a dying baby and a thriving baby. Finally, there are those who can only see your decision as an act of abandonment because of their own buried feelings of rejection. They project their own deep seated pain onto your baby and cannot accept "what you've done." It hits a raw nerve. Naturally those feelings of abandonment and rejection don't belong to your baby, as they would argue, but belong to them. Their difficulty supporting you has nothing to do with you and your decision.

Remind yourself that these people are limited because of simplistic thinking and/or their own emotional issues. Above all, remember this: you don't require their approval to know in your heart that you made the best decision you could, the right decision for your baby. However, especially in the thick of your grief and doubts, it is normal to be upset by their remarks.

Sometimes, not responding to them is a valid option. But particularly if destructive comments come from someone with whom you have an ongoing relationship – friend, relative, neighbor, coworker – it may serve you best to stand up to them. A blanket statement may be effective, such as, **I really need your support, not your harsh judgment.** If you can share your grief and love for your baby, that may also help them understand that your decision was not an act of rejection or evil. Or you can try the following responses to specific remarks:

How could you let your baby die? How could you choose death?
Death was beyond our control. Modern medical technology couldn't offer our baby any cures, so really, we didn't have much of a choice but to let nature take its course.

I would've tried anything to make my baby survive.
For our baby, it would only prolong suffering and/or dying.

What if the diagnosis was wrong?
That doesn't change the fact that our baby died from something that was fatal.

What if the information on treatment options you received from the doctors wasn't accurate? There's this specialist I've heard about. . .
We could only make decisions based on the facts and opinions at hand.

What if your doctors were wrong about your baby's prognosis?
The best we could do was rely on the doctors' years of education and experience, and we had to trust that. We all did the best we could.

You shouldn't have refused/stopped treatment.
I was with my baby, and there was such a sense of peace. You are entitled to your opinion. I am blessed with my knowledge and experience.

You just took the easy way out.
Letting go was the easy way out for my baby. She suffers no more. But for me, left behind to grieve, letting go was the most difficult thing I've ever done.

You were selfish. You just didn't want a handicapped child.
I didn't want my child to be burdened with a minimal, painful, debilitating existence. Deciding to let go, to turn away from aggressive medical intervention and let nature take its course, feels like the most unselfish thing I've ever done.

Maybe if you had kept your baby alive, a miracle would've happened, just like that other baby.
If our baby's life was meant to be miraculously spared, it would have happened while our baby was alive. Miracles don't require the assistance of aggressive medical intervention.

Miracles happen to those who have enough faith.
We have faith in the idea that what happened was supposed to happen, and that our destinies hold many small miracles. Our baby's life was one of those miracles.

What gives you the right to play God and discontinue life support?
Actually, we asked ourselves what would give us the right to play God and *continue* life support. When we disconnected the machines, that's when we placed our baby's life in the hand of God.

What about the right to life?
We believe everyone has a right to autonomy, choice, dignity and peace. The right to life must be linked to those rights. A mere physical existence only mocks life.

What about the sanctity of human life?
We have a deep respect for the preciousness of every individual and the sanctity of human dignity. Sentencing our child to such a limited existence would dishonor those ideals. It is the person who is of value, not physical existence.

I thought euthanasia/mercy killing was against the law.
We did not kill our baby; we allowed our baby to live his natural life and to have a gracious death.

Don't you feel like you killed your baby?
Death was beyond our control. All we did was try to make our baby's life and death as peaceful as we could – by holding her and loving her and letting go instead of prolonging suffering.

Maybe you should have . . .
But the reality is. . ., and that is what we need support for.

If you let your baby die, you must not have loved him enough. I guess it was easy to let your baby die since you weren't bonded yet.
Actually we started loving/bonding to this baby the minute we found out we were pregnant. The grief we feel knows no bounds. This is the most heart-wrenching experience I've ever faced.

If you don't have the presence of mind to respond at the moment, it may be helpful to confront the offenders later. Even if you don't have the nerve to respond in person, write them a note (you don't have to send it), or simply imagine yourself responding to them, leveling them with your conviction. The important thing to remember is not to try to change their views, but to insist that they respect yours. Even if they don't accept your decision, they can refrain from being hurtful to you. If necessary, avoid them while you heal.

Notes. . .

Letting Go . . .

After your baby dies, the process of letting go begins in earnest. Letting go involves grieving and working through your feelings of emptiness, sadness, anger and vulnerability. It is also important to dwell on memories and mementos of your baby so you can experience a gradual goodbye. While your grief will follow a unique path full of unpredictable ups and downs, you can expect it to slowly soften over a period of several years. This may seem like an interminable length of time, but as the months pass, the ups do become more frequent and longer lasting.

Anger, Guilt and Failure

Anger is one of the most prevalent grieving emotions for any bereaved parent. For parents who turned away from aggressive medical intervention, there is a special realm of things to feel angry about. You may feel angry at the medical staff for the way information was presented or avoided. You may resent that such important decisions had to be made with scant information, in so little time and under so much emotional duress. You may bristle when people try to second guess your decision. You may be upset that your baby demanded such a high price for parenthood.

You may feel angry that medicine holds the promise of so much, yet for your baby, it delivered so little. You may feel bitter about the impossible state of medical technology. Its ability to sustain life without regard to quality put you in the awful position of making tough decisions.

You may feel exasperated with your partner if you had an unjust share of the information seeking or decision-making. You may feel furious with God, fate or Mother Nature for handing you such a difficult situation. Most of all, you may feel angry that life is so unfair, that your baby was so sick and had to endure such a short, perhaps painful existence.

This sense of unfairness can be one of the most striking, angry emotions you encounter. It's unfair that your baby had such profound problems. It's unfair that modern medicine couldn't offer any good solutions. Grace remembers feeling how unfair it was that she could not penetrate the technology surrounding her son. *It was heartbreaking to wait every day while one new specialist took a look at James and made his evaluation, when all I really wanted to do was hold James and have someone understand how sad I was that I couldn't even do that.* For Molly, even as she and Ted were trying to reach a decision, what she wanted most was *recognition that it was truly unfair for anyone to make the decision we had to make.*

Anger can also take the form of guilt or failure. You may be angry with yourself for not asking certain questions or for making certain choices. You may wish you had done something differently. You may be disappointed in yourself for not spending more time with your baby, even when doing so led you into the depths of despair. Perhaps, such overwhelming emotion was too much to bear.

These feelings of guilt and failure arise from the belief that you should be in total control of your life. Unfortunately, you can't always avoid tragedy or know the right course of action. No one can. Instead of being angry at yourself for things you did or didn't do, accept that you did the best you could in an impossible situation. Instead of being angry at yourself for decisions you made, be angry that you were put in the position of having to choose between terrible and horrible.

All these angry feelings are natural and common. As you grieve, it is important to acknowledge and express your angry feelings in constructive ways. Try talking about them to a supportive person, writing them down or drawing pictures. Try physical releases such as crying, active sports, pounding pillows or relaxation techniques. Anger can be a powerful and scary feeling, but by acknowledging and releasing it, you avoid the damage it can do. If you keep it bottled up inside, you increase its power to burst or slither out in ways that hurt you or others.

Finding Treasure in Adversity

In spite of the impossible situation you faced, you may feel a sense of having played an intense, indispensable role in your baby's life. For most parents, decisions weighing the *best interests of the child* don't get much more serious than choosing between cloth and synthetic diapers, private or public schooling. Choosing between nature and medical technology is surely one of the most passionate parenting experiences. As a result, your relationship with this child was extraordinarily profound and poignant, concentrated and heartfelt.

Perhaps you will always resent having to make this decision. But if you can discover some positives, you will be able to more easily find meaning and integrate this experience into your life. Integration comes with embracing the lessons learned, uncovering the blessings, and focusing on the love. As you grieve, you are also healing, and when you are ready, you will find the treasure.

This whole experience tore me apart. It has also had a profound effect on my life. I treasure life more that I ever did.

Lena

For quite some time, I was angry that with all the technology, they could save tiny two pound babies but not my big healthy nine pound, thirteen ouncer. I now feel that without that technology, Mark would have been stillborn and I'm very grateful for the 5 1/2 days I did have with him, to be his mother, and to cherish that relationship.

Beth

. . . With Love

Part of being a parent is discovering that remarkable feeling of devotion to your child's welfare and happiness. Lena recalls, *My sister told me that once you have your baby, if someone told you to step in front of a train to save your baby's life, you wouldn't even think twice and you'd do it. I didn't believe her at the time. Now I do.* When faced with a very sick baby, however, that commitment is intensified. The situation isn't hypothetical and the solutions aren't as simple as stepping in front of a train, much less guaranteed. Claudia remembers her own extraordinary feelings of devotion, *If there was something I physically could've done to save his life, if I could've given him my heart, I really think at that point, the place I was in then, I might have done that.*

Another expression of parental devotion is accepting the child for the very one she or he is. In essence, letting nature take its course is an act of total acceptance – of the child's strengths and weaknesses, beauty and imperfections, potential and fate. This isn't to say that parents shouldn't opt for medical intervention if it offers their baby health and wholeness. But if a baby's problems are beyond medicine's reach, then refusing intervention says, *You are precious and I accept the way you are, body and soul. I decline to try to mold you into someone else.*

One more gesture of devotion is a parent's ability to let go. Normally, letting go is a drawn out process that involves giving up control, trusting the child to find his or her own path through life, allowing him to make mistakes and learn from them, and giving her room to grow into a responsible, independent person. From encouraging a toddler to pick out her own clothes to permitting a teenager to date, parents normally have many years to give their child both roots and wings. But when the letting go involves death, particularly so soon after birth, it can be incredibly traumatic.

As such, deciding to turn away from aggressive medical intervention can be the ultimate act of parental devotion. The urge to protect and hold onto your baby at all costs can be so strong, and yet your sense of what is best for your child prevailed upon you to give your child wings. This takes a lot of courage and faith. And as John points out, *I really view it as probably the most unselfish thing that I've ever done.*

Accepting and Moving On

At first, your baby's death is something you do not want to accept. Letting go is something you cannot do all at once. Given the alternatives, you did decide it was best to let your baby be, to concede to the fate that awaited. But your concession probably felt more like a surrender under protest than a graceful acquiescence. Even after your decisions, you may have resisted the idea that your baby would die until the very end.

Grieving is what enables you to come to terms with your baby's illness, your decision and your baby's death. Eventually, you will learn to accept and integrate this experience into your life. As you adjust and find peace, letting go will feel more comfortable.

To adjust and heal, you must go through the grieving process, that is, work through your sadness, anger, hurt and other painful feelings. By dwelling on your memories and emotions, eventually, you will discover that you can remember your baby without falling apart. As you adjust, your sadness and longing will mellow and merge with happier memories. You can accept that your relationship with your baby has changed and you acquire a sense of peace. Although you move on, you take your memories with you, and you will always keep a place in your heart for this baby.

As you grieve, be kind to yourself. Give yourself permission to fall apart, to give up responsibilities, to withdraw, to spend time alone with just your feelings and your memories. Do what you need to do to feel close to your baby and to say your good-byes. Take all the time you need.

I miss James. There are days when well-meaning acquaintances glee-fully show me pictures of their baby boys and I smile for them and cry inside. It hurts. It hurts to see healthy, thriving life when on days like today I want James back, with all his imperfections and all his peaceful presence. I want to talk to those same acquaintances about my son, the light that was in my life for twenty-seven days and pass them my pic-tures of a child who now has another home, another form. They would be offended, most likely, to see pictures of a dead child. But to me, the most important part of James never died. It's that part I can touch occa-sionally now when I think of him. It's that calm, peaceful acceptance of what is, that mystery of life, that power of love, acceptance of someone for who they truly are, that I recall when I think of James. And that will never die.

Grace

Selected References

Medical Ethics, Decision-Making, Palliative Care

Anspach, R. R. *Deciding Who Lives: Fateful Choices in the Intensive Care Nursery.* Berkeley: University of California Press, 1997.

Carter, BS, Levetown M (Eds.) *Palliative Care for Infants, Children, and Adolescents.* Baltimore: Johns Hopkins University Press, 2004.

Children's Project on Palliative/Hospice Services (ChiPPS.) *Compendium of Pediatric Palliative Care.* Alexandria, VA: NHPCO, 2002. www.nhpco.org

Dailey AA, Zarbock S (Eds.) *Hospice Care for Children* (2nd edition.) New York: Oxford University Press, 2001.

Davis, D. L. *Loving and Letting Go: For Bereaved Parents Who Turned Away from Aggressive Medical Intervention for Their Critically Ill Newborn.* Rev. ed. Omaha: Centering, 2002.

Goldman A, Hain R, Liben S. *Oxford Texbook of Palliative Care for Children.* Oxford: Oxford University Press, 2006.

Ellenchild Pinch, W. J. *When the Bough Breaks: Parental Perceptions of Ethical Decision-Making in NICU.* Lanham, Md.: University Press of America, 2002.

Guyer, R.L. *Baby at Risk: The Uncertain Legacies of Medical Miracles for Babies, Families, and Society.* Sterling, Virginia: Capital Books, 2006.

Lantos, J. D. *The Lazarus Case: Life-and-Death Issues in Neonatal Intensive Care.* Baltimore: Johns Hopkins University Press, 2001.

Lyon, J. *Playing God in the Nursery.* New York: W. W. Norton, 1985.

Personal Stories:

Alecson, D. *Lost Lullaby.* Berkeley: University of California Press, 1995. A personal account: medical ethics and parental rights to decline medical intervention for a baby whose prognosis is grim.

Butler, M. *Born to Die?* Dublin: Marino Books, 1995. A mother's personal account: making difficult medical decisions; overcoming ambivalent feelings toward her baby whose prognosis is poor.

Kuebelbeck, A. *Waiting with Gabriel: A Story of Cherishing a Baby's Brief Life.* Chicago: Loyola Press, 2002.

Kay, R. *Saul.* New York: St. Martin's Press, 2000.

Loizeaux, W. Anna: *A Daughter's Life.* New York: Arcade Publishing, 1993.

Mehren, E. *Born Too Soon: The Story of Emily, Our Premature Baby.* New York: Doubleday, 1991.

Neonatal Guidelines for Parents and Health Care Professionals
The Colorado Collective for Medical Decisions

The Colorado Collective for Medical Decisions (CCMD) was a group of concerned health care professionals, parents and community members across Colorado who worked together over the course of about 5 years (1994 to 1999), in order to create community-based guidelines that addressed medical care and end-of-life decision-making. To address the medical care of critically ill newborns, CCMD created the Neonatal Guidelines and Neonatal Video "You Are Not Alone." Our goal in developing community-based guidelines was to serve the following purposes:

- To promote open community discussion around difficult NICU medical/ethical issues in the hope that these medical resources and technology will be used wisely and humanely;

- To encourage and enhance the dialogue between the parents and health care professionals during this difficult, heart-wrenching time;

- To empower physicians to be decision leaders when a baby's prognosis is clear, whether poor or favorable;

- To facilitate collaborative decision-making between health care providers and the parents of critically ill newborns for whom the prognosis is unclear;

- To support parents emotionally, whatever decision they make for their babies;

- To remind outsiders that they must be fully informed about the specific medical realities before voicing an opinion about treatment choices or attempting to represent the best interests of any infant.

CCMD Neonatal Guidelines

Modern medical technology achieves many good and important goals. A primary goal of neonatal intensive care is to help sick infants become healthy children.

To use technology wisely, we must acknowledge its limitations. For some infants, the burdens of treatment outweigh the benefits.

Parents must be fully informed about the risks, benefits, outcomes and uncertainties of aggressive medical intervention for their individual baby. Whether an infant lives or dies, it is the parents who ultimately live with the result.

When the prognosis is clear, health care providers should be decision leaders.

When the prognosis is unclear (or becomes unclear), health care providers should work collaboratively with parents as decisions are made about an infant's care.

When aggressive intervention is withheld or withdrawn, comfort care should be provided.

When aggressive intervention is pursued for an infant whose outcome is uncertain, physicians should discuss with parents the specific burdens of treatment, and how benefits and outcomes remain speculative.

For all NICU infants, regular and timely care conferences between parents and health care teams are an integral part of providing appropriate treatment.

Follow-up care should be provided to all families.

CCMD Neonatal Videotape

The videotape *You Are Not Alone* was designed to support parents and enhance parent-professional communication when a newborn infant has a poor or uncertain prognosis.

CCMD Guidelines featured as written text in the video:

Infants who are likely to survive should be given appropriate medical care even if they have mental or physical limitations.

Infants who are extremely unlikely to survive infancy due to extreme prematurity should receive comfort care instead of aggressive life-sustaining interventions.

Infants who are extremely unlikely to survive infancy due to a lethal birth defect should receive comfort care instead of aggressive life-sustaining interventions.

Infants for whom survival offers only a short lifetime filled with significant suffering should receive comfort care instead of life-sustaining interventions.

When the outcome of aggressive medical care for an infant is uncertain, the family should be provided with comprehensive information about outcomes.

When the outcome of aggressive medical care for an infant is uncertain, decisions about life-sustaining interventions should be made jointly by the family and medical team.

Please copy and distribute CCMD guidelines.

To obtain copies of the CCMD neonatal videotape, *You Are Not Alone,* please contact:
Nickel's Worth Productions
(303) 825-5555   NickelTV@aol.com

Each video includes written materials that describe the video's intended uses, offer guidance for providing support to parents and involving them in decision-making, plus the CCMD Neonatal Guidelines for medical decision-making in the NICU.

About the Author

Deborah L. Davis, Ph.D., is a developmental psychologist who specializes in perinatal and neonatal crisis, medical ethics, parental bereavement, parent education and child development. As a member of the Colorado Collective for Medical Decisions, she collaborated on writing the Neonatal Guidelines, which supports ethical and humane decision-making in the NICU. She is also a member of the National NICU Advisory Committee for the March of Dimes NICU Pilot Project, and she collaborated on writing the booklet, **Parent: You & Your Baby in the NICU**. Dr. Davis is the author of four books for bereaved parents, **Empty Cradle, Broken Heart** (Fulcrum, 1991; 1996), **Loving and Letting Go** (Centering,1993; 2002), **Fly Away Home** (Centering, 2000), and **Stillbirth, Yet Still Born** (PILC, 2000). Currently, she is writing a book with Mara Tesler Stein, Psy.D., entitled **The Emotional Journey of Parenting Your Premature Baby: A Book of Hope and Healing** (NICU Ink).

Debbie's book, **Empty Cradle, Broken Heart**, contains much additional supportive information on the many feelings that accompany the death of a baby, as well as comfort and reassurance in the quotes of other parents who have been there. Your feelings are normal, and you are not alone.

Debbie has written another book for Centering that addresses life-and-death decisions for older babies and children, entitled **Fly Away Home: For Bereaved Parents Who Turned Away from Aggressive Medical Intervention for Their Critically Ill Child.** Like **Loving and Letting Go**, this gentle book asserts the wise and humane use of medical technology and affirms for parents that their decisions come from love, devotion and the courage to let their beloved child *fly away home*.

Contact:
Centering Corporation
PO Box 4600
Omaha, NE 68104
Phone: 402-553-1200

Remember that grief is not a sign of weakness. Rather, it takes strength and courage to acknowledge your emotions. This is a time to listen to your feelings, to nurture yourself, to value yourself, to get the emotional support you need.
From: **Empty Cradle, Broken Heart**